Kent

Edited By Sarah Olivo

First published in Great Britain in 2019 by:

Young Writers
Remus House
Coltsfoot Drive
Peterborough
PE2 9BF
Telephone: 01733 890066
Website: www.youngwriters.co.uk

Book Design by Ashley Janson

SB ISBN 978-1-78988-030-4
Printed and bound in the UK by BookPrintingUK
Website: www.bookprintinguk.com
YB0385J

FOREWORD

Here at Young Writers, we love to let imaginations run wild and creativity go crazy. Our aim is to encourage young people to get their creative juices flowing and put pen to paper. Each competition is tailored to the relevant age group, hopefully giving each pupil the inspiration and incentive to create their own piece of creative writing, whether it's a poem or a short story. By allowing them to see their own work in print, we know their confidence and love for the written word will grow.

For our latest competition Poetry Wonderland, we invited primary school pupils to create wild and wonderful poems on any topic they liked – the only limits were the limits of their imagination! Using poetry as their magic wand, these young poets have conjured up worlds, creatures and situations that will amaze and astound or scare and startle! Using a variety of poetic forms of their own choosing, they have allowed us to get a glimpse into their vivid imaginations. We hope you enjoy wandering through the wonders of this book as much as we have.

CONTENTS

High Firs Primary School, Swanley

Hilden Grange School, Tonbridge

Kings Hill School, Kings Hill

Selling CE Primary School, Selling

Small Haven Independent Special Needs School, Ramsgate

Snodland CE Primary School, Snodland

St James' CE Primary Academy, Isle Of Grain

St Peter's Catholic Primary School, Sittingbourne

Temple Hill Primary Academy, Dartford

The Poems

Winter Wind Funtime

W inter is quiet, shivering, cold
I n winter, it starts to get more and more cold
N early everyone is playing in the snow
T he snow is quite cold
E veryone likes the cold snow
R ight now, people are making snowy white snowmen

W inter is fun to play in
I n the cold, a snowy day
N o one can resist the snow
D ays with snow are fun

F inally, winter's nearly finished
U ntil that's done, we will enjoy the snow
N o one is happy that the snow's going
T he fun snow is great
I would like to see the snow
M e and my friends love to play in the snow
E veryone will say goodbye to the snow.

Amber Kristina Jenkins (7)
Belvedere Junior School, Belvedere

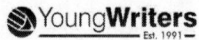

The Crumble Problem

There was a man in a hat
who wanted to have some crumble.
He went to the baker's shop
to get some crumble.
Mmm, yum yum!
The man went back to the house with excitement
he went to get a spoon.
When he turned around
the crumble went *boom*
like a moon!
Exploded was his crumble
what trouble!
Trouble crumble
what a muddle
a crumble muddle!
He swept up the crumble.
Back to the baker's shop.
He had some more crumble.
He went to get his spoon
shaped like a moon.

The man turned around
to see his crumble getting into trouble.
He had forgot all about something
he had visitors!
The man in the hat
went to the cat
the cat looked at the map
the map in the gap.
The cat put on a strap
and strode to the bakery.
"Crumble, please."
At home, the man in the hat
had his spoon ready.
"Let's eat, my friend!"
They were best friends forever
forever together!

Jaymee Moukouono (7)
Belvedere Junior School, Belvedere

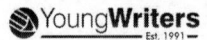

The Car Who Had Cheese In Tea

Once, there lived a car
not any other car
but the car princess
who couldn't travel very far.

She was the slowest, but one of the prettiest
she was the least athletic, but one of the wittiest
she was bullied and misled
but she was the princess!

One day, she was up to her back tyres
she packed her belongings and set off far away
after no longer than an hour, she reached a café
inside smelt of pastry and coffee, but most of all of cheese
she drove in with a sigh of relief and ordered a tea
a tea with cheese? Quite odd, if you ask me.

The unique order was delivered
and so the princess drank and shivered

in the process, she made a friend
by being herself and no one else.

Favour Chinenye Nwadikeduruibe (10)

Belvedere Junior School, Belvedere

Wonderland

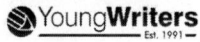

The treasure chest
Is full of gold
With all the stories
Yet to be told

Enchanted trees stand
Straight and tall
Which makes everything else
Look very small

Little monsters flying around
Being cheeky and sneaky
Making snorting sounds

Rainbow rockets zooming in the sky
Around burger planets and
Chocolate mushrooms wrapped in bow ties

Skies of purple
Emerald leaves
Who knows what kind of magic
Is up your sleeves?

So if you're ever looking
For candle stars
Or butterflies made
Out of bread

Don't look them up on your screens
Go to Wonderland instead.

Brooke Cheriton (11)
Belvedere Junior School, Belvedere

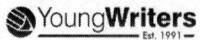

Learn To Fry A Baby Elf On Mars

I learnt how to fry a baby elf.
I could see the barbeque crackling
and the crisps flipping on Planet Mars
and I saw the aliens playing with a giant hopscotch.
I could hear the chocolate singing
and the cheese sunbathing on Mars.
I could feel the yummy cheeseburger.
Just when I was going to eat it
an alien jumped out of the hole
and took my cheeseburger.
I could hear the rabbit falling down the hole on Mars.
I could feel the elf dancing in my hand.
I could see the smelly smoke coming out of his nose.
I could hear the boogeys bouncing on the floor on Planet Mars.
The aliens were jumping to get the boogeys.

Andre Foong (7)
Belvedere Junior School, Belvedere

The Hungry Lion

The lion is happy
He is furry and fluffy
But his fur is smelly and deadly
None of the animals dare to laugh

The lion is hungry and angry
He roars as loud as an elephant
He falls asleep, he's floppy and sleepy
But nobody knows what he will do when he wakes up.

He wakes up
The lion starts to cry with tears
Drip-drop, down his face
Hungry and sad, he goes back to the jungle.

The animals wait and stay until the lion is there
He is back, he is sleepy and tired
All the animals dance and prance
They've brought food and water for the sleepy, hungry lion.

Zelekah Broderick (8)
Belvedere Junior School, Belvedere

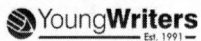

World War II Invasion Has Begun

Being held against their will,
Trying not to kill.
Guns being shot,
Don't want to get the chop.
I want to be strong,
Home is where I belong.
Will there be a home?
Or will I be alone?
Distorted and stressed,
Thinking of what I care about best.
I want to see my family and my friends,
I want to stick it out 'til the very end.
I go to the officer.
I hate the destruction here.
Counting down the days 'til Christmas.
Don't know how I will get through this.
I will be strong,
I will move on,
So remembrance is all I need.

I will be strong,
I will move on.

Rushil Jigen Patel (10)
Belvedere Junior School, Belvedere

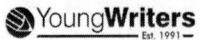

Space Adventure

I am an alien
as mean as can be
I am going to find a pet to help me
so don't try to stop me from destroying you
because my pet, Rocky
will make a ray gun to shrink you.

When you get destroyed
be careful, I will eat you
I will, don't make me drink you instead.

My pet may be a rock
but he will hurt you when I train him
he is as hard as can be
if he breaks
I will work alone.

No one can destroy me
no one.

I must have a feast
maybe turkey
or maybe you!

I will use your bones for a trophy
and your meat for dinner.

Ryan Thomas (9)
Belvedere Junior School, Belvedere

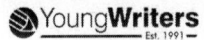

My Favourite Animals

Puppy, puppy, you're so cute,
Puppy, puppy, you walk so slow,
Puppy, puppy, fetch that stick,
Puppy, puppy, drink your water.

Fishy, fishy, swim so slow,
Fishy, fishy, play so fast,
Fishy, fishy, eat your rotten food,
Fishy, fishy, get eaten by the shark.

Monkey, monkey, jump and swing,
Monkey, monkey, be crazy and lazy,
Monkey, monkey, eat some banana pyjamas,
Monkey, monkey, why are you so cheeky, sneaky?

Lion, lion, hear him roar,
Lion, lion, you always want more,
You are always sneaky when prey is near,
You hunt beasts without fear.

Jasleen Sandhu (8)
Belvedere Junior School, Belvedere

My Lion

My incredible lion is very fast.
The lion never comes last.
As loud as nuclear bombs, *roar!*
The awesome creature raises its paw.
My lion eats the meat.
The lion bites my metal even though it is rusty.
My pet lion sees my parrot.
I give my lion some tasty food.
My lion stares at me!
Then as loud as a strike of thunder, *roar!*
The fierce lion runs fast
As he can really run fast!
He is faster than a motorbike!
My lion is not a cheetah.
I got my lion in South Africa.
My lion is like my brother.
The incredible lion is my royal guard.

Rylee Nabuufu (8)
Belvedere Junior School, Belvedere

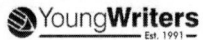

Poem About Animals

Lion, lion, hear the roars,
You hunt without a fear,
Lion, lion, you always want more,
You're always sneaky when prey is near.

Lion, lion, roar so loud,
Lion eats like a monster,
You're a scary, fire-golden lion.

You strike and kill if someone attacks,
You're like a roaring machine,
You run like a hundred cheetahs,
When you roar, the ground shakes and no one is to be seen.

You're a hairy, scary creature,
You're a king and you have golden mane,
You scare everyone away,
You're the king, forever you will reign.

Sarah Lucas (8)
Belvedere Junior School, Belvedere

A Feature Of Animals

Panda, panda, you're so sweet,
You deserve a delicious treat,
Panda, panda, you're so cute,
You're wearing black boots.

Leopard, leopard, with your spots so black,
You are running on the track,
Leopard, you are so fast,
You, Leopard, have done your task.

Tiger, you are covered in stripes,
You are one of a type,
Tiger, you are as fearless as a knight,
You are always right.

Penguin, penguin, you're as cold as ice,
You are very nice,
Penguin sometimes like to harm us and bite,
With its surprising might.

Maya-Louise Odoch (8)
Belvedere Junior School, Belvedere

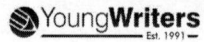

Family And Friends

My mum was making scrambled egg with Simon.
I went in the car that was shiny
and it was the best
it had so much power.
My dad went to work
and then he brought crunchy crisps.
We have big, tall paper
that he brings back
from his adventure.
He brings a shell
and pebble.
We have Great-Great-Grandma
she plays Scrabble
and my favourite game of all time is the Wii.
Last but not least
my aunts.
They make roast and chicken
and my friends play with me all the time
on Xbox and PS4.
Then it is time
to nap, nap, nap...

Mackenzie Aligboro (8)
Belvedere Junior School, Belvedere

Unimaid

Mermaid body, unicorn horn
lives under the sea
and uses magic from her horn.
Eyes turn from purple
to green, to blue, to pink
depending on the feeling she has.
Her horn turns from galaxy
to majestic pink
depending on the time.
She can fly
she can sing
she's the perfect pet for you.
She can do anything you want.
Trust me
this animal is the best
it's the one thing that can change its colour
to the feeling it has.
She can transform into anything you want
from a bird
to a wolf
to a mythical creature.

Julianna Wiecek (10)
Belvedere Junior School, Belvedere

Space

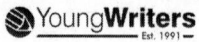

Space is a beautiful place,
A whole different world,
So far,
So cool.

Planets that circle our sun,
Are different in all sorts of ways,
Saturn and its rings,
Mars, the Red Planet,
Some with a moon or thirty-two,
Sometimes full,
Sometimes new.

The black holes,
Taking in all beautiful things,
I can understand,
Would you like this beautiful masterpiece?

Well...
I have to say this,
But there is no safe place in space.
Who knows who or what is out there?

In this place,
Called space.

Courtney Goldsmith (9)
Belvedere Junior School, Belvedere

Monkey

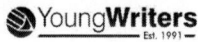

Monkey, monkey, see them party,
Monkey, monkey, acting super naughty,
You see them swing on branches,
You watch them jump on benches.

Monkey, monkey, without long tails,
Monkey, monkey, makes a lot of trails,
You may see them be crazy,
You might find them sleeping lazily.

Monkey, monkey, being so sneaky,
Monkey, monkey, always cheeky,
You will see them eat bananas,
You may see them wear their pyjamas.

Monkey, monkey, always climbs on trees,
Monkey, monkey, always being free,
You can see them without fail.

Micah Basola (8)
Belvedere Junior School, Belvedere

Animals

Monkey, monkey, you are sneaky,
Monkey, monkey, you are cheeky.
You are always singing and swinging,
You are sneaky when you are jumping.

Wolf, never, ever have fear.
Wolf, wolves are always near.
It's always with its pack,
It always comes to attack.

Lion, lion, you don't scare, but you roar,
Lion, lion, don't do more,
If you are so hairy,
Why are you so scary?

Cat, why are you always on the mat?
You always sit in your bed, curling.
Cat, why are you so fat?
You fat cat, stop purring.

Chloe Sandra Rose Bowden (8)
Belvedere Junior School, Belvedere

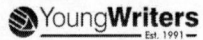

Winter, Christmas

Within winter is Christmas,
Santa coming to give you presents,
but not just any presents,
the presents you want.

In the sky,
you can see soft white snow,
landing on your coat,
and the floor.

No one wants to steal Christmas,
but if someone did,
everyone would be heartbroken,
everyone sad.

To get a present,
you must be good,
listen to adults,
be kind always.

Every year, you must be good,
be kind and be helpful,

restart, have a new beginning,
forget the bad things.

David Osikoya (8)
Belvedere Junior School, Belvedere

Keep Dreaming On

W ishing to dream big is always better,
O nly dream as you want, not as other people want you to,
N ever don't believe your dream will happen, because it could,
D on't ever give up on your dream,
E nter your dreams, big or small,
R ainbows and unicorns never stop dreaming,
L and on a candyfloss cloud,
A nd you could even dream of having a picnic on the moon,
N ow listen here to what I have to say: never stop dreaming,
D ream big or go home, that's what I say.

Liza Cooper (10)
Belvedere Junior School, Belvedere

All About Lions

This creature is really strong!
The creature isn't really long.
Then in a flash, he's gone!
The lion is really brave.

Lions aren't the world's slave.
They are never in a wave!
In a race, he would never be last!

The lion lifted its head and roared!
The lion is on a tour.
The lion is really fierce!
The lion's claws don't pierce.

The lion is really yellow.
Some lions live in meadows.
Lions don't get any letters.
Lions really think they're better.

Raniesha Courtney Mukalazi (8)
Belvedere Junior School, Belvedere

The Poem Of The Jungle

The lion is very hungry,
So the lion is getting angry,
Then he starts roaring,
As he's roaring, he's smelling.

The lion is very brave,
So he goes into his cave,
The lion is getting sleepy,
So he starts to get floppy.

The lion undercover, no tigers he spies,
Lion's jumping into the sky,
The lion, sometimes fast,
They can remember the past.

The lion is very hairy,
Soon starts to get scary,
The lion is very deadly,
So he's smelly.

Ryan Sehra (8)
Belvedere Junior School, Belvedere

Jump On A Flying, Mysterious Shark

I'm on a wonderful island of presents and elves.
Wow! Is that money from the clouds?
Wow! That's a wonderful shark
out in the wonderful, blue, shiny sea
that sounds fun!
Should I jump on the shark's back
because it's a blue, colourful, big shark...?
Yes, now I've made it
so I need to make it go to sleep
so I need to say a rhyme.
"It's time to go below ice
slow done, shutdown, shutdown..."
Now I jump
ah, wow, I'm flying
this is fun!

Max Walker (7)

Belvedere Junior School, Belvedere

Overload Omniverse

Once, someone went to a garden
and they planted crops
then one crop turned into a dragon
and another into a gauntlet.
He used the gauntlet on the dragon
and he eventually turned into a dragon
so he was a superhero!
Secretly, the gauntlet was getting overloaded with DNA
then he zapped a volcano
and the gauntlet burned.
All that was left
were its cores.
He ate the cores
time, reality, ice, speed.
He got more superpowers
but the superpowers faded...

Osaro Brian Avuvu (8)
Belvedere Junior School, Belvedere

My Space Journey

I once went into space in a hot-air balloon
But when I got there, the sun was too hot and popped my balloon.
I was stuck on Mercury and didn't know what to do.
I heard that there was a magic powder that could get me home soon
So I went to search the planets and found it on the moon.
Then I took it back to my balloon
I fixed it up and jumped back on
So sad to go, it was so much fun
Not enough time did I get
Next time, I will take a jumbo jet.

Summer Lloyd (9)
Belvedere Junior School, Belvedere

King Of The Animals - Lion!

The lion is as sleepy
as the magnificent sky.
A lion is very scary
but so very, very hairy.

A lion's mane is huffy
and is ever so puffy.
A lion's ears are very floppy
it loves being hoppy.

When a lion is hungry
it roars and gets angry.
A lion is as sly
as a terrible, deadly sacrifice.

A lion is as scary
as a tiger, so hairy.
A lion is as fierce
as a claw that can pierce.

Layla Ong (8)
Belvedere Junior School, Belvedere

Space Is Not Like Anything Else...

Space is amazing,
the most amazing thing ever.

Space is wonderful,
it will be there forever.

Space isn't big,
space isn't gigantic,
space isn't enormous,
space is much, much more!

Space is cool,
as cool as your sunglasses.

Space is great,
as great as Jupiter's gases.

Space is beautiful,
the planets themselves,
space is not like anything else...

Prajina Gopikishna (10)
Belvedere Junior School, Belvedere

A Pigeon Called Perry

Perry flew so fast
he bumped his head
now Perry thinks
he's a peregrine falcon instead.

So he tries to fly high
in the bright blue sky
looking for his new friends
he just wants to say, "Hi!"

"Can't see them up here..."
He's agile
so dives from up high
but when he tries
he doesn't see what comes from behind...

Grab! Squawk! Gulp!

Zachary Derry (7)
Belvedere Junior School, Belvedere

My Moon!

You are my night star,
you are my night soul.

Looking at the moon tonight,
oh, what a sight.

When the stars shine upon you,
my moon.

But when you go, you leave me with a frown,
but when you come back, I rush to see you!

You are my night star,
you are my night soul.

Looking at the moon tonight,
oh, what a sight.

When the stars shine upon you,
my moon!

Teddy Catlin-Johnstone (9)
Belvedere Junior School, Belvedere

Christmas

Christmas is coming
Christmas is here
Ready or not
Seasonal greetings
Hope and love
Christmas is here

Christmas is coming
Cooking and baking
Sharing and wishing
Thanks and giving
Ready or not
Christmas is here

Christmas is coming
Fun is coming
Snow is pouring
Children playing, having fun
Ready or not
Christmas is here
Hmm! I love Christmas!

Carys Thompson (7)
Belvedere Junior School, Belvedere

The Sorting Hat!

You might belong in Gryffindor,
Where they fight for the best,
And stay brave no matter what;

You might belong in Hufflepuff,
Where they are loyal to others,
And truly not afraid of hard work;

Or yet in wise old Ravenclaw,
Always ready minds,
And will master all tests;

Or perhaps in Slytherin,
Potions and history is their thing,
And they try to achieve to the end.

Nicola Fichardo (10)
Belvedere Junior School, Belvedere

The King Of The Lions

The lion is very floppy.
The lion is very hungry.
The lion is very hairy.
The lion is very angry.

The lion is the king.
The lion is very scary.
The lion is sly.
The lion is very vicious.

The lion is very fluffy.
The lion is very smily.
The lion is very brave.
The lion is very monotonous.

The lion is very deluded.
The lion is very dangerous.

Ruby King (8)
Belvedere Junior School, Belvedere

We're Going To The Moon

Climb aboard the spaceship,
We're going to the moon,
Hurry,
Get ready,
We're to blast-off soon,
Now wear your helmets and buckle up tight,
And no eating food until,
It's dark at night,
Jokes, it's always day and night, as long as you're in space,
Because now we're in space,
So feel the sun burn on,
Your happy, smiley, melting face.

Aseemah Oreoluwa Okin (9)
Belvedere Junior School, Belvedere

The Lion Roar

The lion raised its fluffy paw
Then the creature snuck up and roared!
He runs like a creature very fast
And in a race, he's never last.

The lion is very brave
And he lives in a cave
And the lion is very clever
And he likes the weather.

The lion is like a blast!
Then he's very fast
If he's so fast
He can go to the past!

Billy Seaman Thomas Nicholls (8)
Belvedere Junior School, Belvedere

The Bombs Are Going

The bombs are ticking
gotta get out.
Nowhere to run, nowhere to hide.
I need to defuse the bombs.
Knife or some scissors will do
but there are none in the room.
I see a hatch on the floor
I look in and there is an ice cream land
and I get in.
The bomb goes off
and I live!
I get up
all bombs are gone.
The door is blown open...

Dylan Anthony Pearce (8)
Belvedere Junior School, Belvedere

The Fearless Wolf

Wolf is searching the hills,
Wolf, wolf, likes to howl,
You are always wanting to kill,
You like to eat owl.

Wolf, you protect your den,
Wolf, you have no fear,
You love to eat hen,
You will need prey near.

Wolf, you love your pack,
Wolf, wolf, attack your prey.
You can go to attack predators,
You and your pack stay.

Lucas Suter (8)
Belvedere Junior School, Belvedere

Bears

Bears hunt when prey is near,
They walk in the woods without fear,
They're big and they're furry,
They never, ever, ever worry.

Bears don't ever say sorry,
They always hurry,
Most of them are chubby,
They like to rub and scratch their hands around their tummy.

They have a huge body,
They never cry for their mummy.

Oreoluwa Adisa (8)
Belvedere Junior School, Belvedere

The Scary Lion

Lion, lion, hear you roar,
Lion, eat some more.
You bounce as you pounce,
You never hunt with fear.

Lion, lion, always super fiesty,
You drive us insane with your mane.
Lion, lion, so hairy and scary,
You'll always be king.

Lion, lion, you always act mighty,
Lion, lion, get anything near,
You are always a beast.

Berrin Akin (8)
Belvedere Junior School, Belvedere

The Kite

I
fly
so high
in the sky
brightly dyed
I soar and glide
the wind is my guide
as I flutter and enthrall
when I face a squall
although I'm small
I'm visible to all
ecstatically
everybody
can see
me.

I scan the beautiful skyline
I dance in the warm sunshine
and go all the way up.

Jasmine Kaur Dhanju (10)
Belvedere Junior School, Belvedere

Lion, Lion

Lion, lion, hear him roar
Lion, lion, you always want more
You are always sneaky when prey is near
You hunt beasts without fear.

Lion, lion, bright as gold
Lion, lion, king of all
You are mighty, but feisty too
You are hairy like grass.

Lion, lion, loud as a horn
Lion, lion, you don't sing, but you roar.

Gabrielius Makarevicius (8)
Belvedere Junior School, Belvedere

The King

The king with his sharp teeth
to poke the zebra with a grin
and suck its blood with his teeth
he's cool and he likes to rule.

The king of the jungle
is losing his life
he can't hold onto his wife.

The king is in danger
we have to help him
so he doesn't go away
for a day.

Amari Hyatt (9)
Belvedere Junior School, Belvedere

Princess Perfect

S parkly glitter,
T winkly stars!
E pic gown,
L oving it!
L ittle rays,
A gain, again,
S himmering carnations, pink and white!

R oses blossom,
O leander scent!
S uper soft morning glories everywhere!
E rica Land.

Sadie Sahid (10)
Belvedere Junior School, Belvedere

Bear, Bear

Bear, bear, don't you glare,
Bear, bear, your mission is to scare,
All the other animals run in fear,
When they hear you near.

Bear, bear, with your mighty paws and jaws.
I hear in the distance your mighty roars,
Time for your favourite dish,
It will always be fish.

Rina Kaur Bhandal (8)
Belvedere Junior School, Belvedere

A Little Girl's Dream

A little girl's dream,
I'm thinking about giant, glittery ice cream,
With me flying on a unicorn across the sky,
Oh so very high,
I'm thinking you should too,
I really hope this comes true,
I hate monsters,
I hate bugs,
And I definitely hate slugs.

Marykate Nicholls (10)
Belvedere Junior School, Belvedere

The Dinosaur

In Sidedia was found an unnatural dinosaur,
He had eyes like an onion and a very wide tongue.
He had a big horn that reached the sea.
He had big teeth of ice and ate only the green.
He had small arms and only gathered leaves.
Now I wonder if this dinosaur could fly!

Sebastian Valentin Batcá (10)
Belvedere Junior School, Belvedere

The Lion And Monkey Poem

Lion, lion, hear him sing,
Lion, lion, he's always king,
He is always hairy,
And after all, he's very scary

Monkey, monkey, you're very jumpy,
Monkey, monkey, you're always bumpy,
You're always hairy,
But you're never scary.

Joseph Emmanuel (8)
Belvedere Junior School, Belvedere

Leopard

A leopard's spots are a leopard's beauty.
A leopard is as fast as a cheetah.
A leopard lies under a tree.
A leopard has sharp jaws.
A leopard has fluffy hair.
A leopard has great hunting skill.

A leopard.

Kayden Eve (7)
Belvedere Junior School, Belvedere

Potion Making

Witches and wizards throwing this and that,
Adding a rat and a bat,
Making it green, blue, purple and red,
"This will make it yellow," the witches said,
Checking the shelves up and down,
Quickly going to town,
Buying some spider legs,
Swiftly going home and hanging their robes on pegs,
Dumping it all in the cupboard,
"Now this will be explosive!" the wizards shuddered,
Suddenly, there was an enormous *bang* and blast,
The witches laughed, "We shouldn't have done it that fast!"
At least the potion was fit,
The wizards said, "Let's drink most of it!"
Lucky them, they wouldn't ever be ill!

Muhammad Abdul Hadi Siddique (9)
Fleetdown Primary School, Dartford

How My Dinner Party Went Wrong

I was meant to host a dinner party,
With all my lovely friends.
My food was fun and hearty,
Everyone loved it, well that depends.
For dessert we had green jelly,
That was when I made the wrong choice.
Everyone left with a full belly,
Just then I heard a voice.
Beware, beware of the jelly thingy,
My fluffy dog came along and shook the table.
Suddenly, appeared a monster that was gooey and springy,
It must have come from the dinner party.
There's a myth about this and jelly being sour,
However, my jelly was not at all tarty.
It was there for over an hour,
And I don't know what to do with it.

Angel Dai (10)
Fleetdown Primary School, Dartford

Prison Escape

The doors have opened for our break,
This escape will be a piece of cake.
I hoisted up the long thick rope,
And then I felt a very sharp poke.
I turned around and saw a cop,
He grabbed me by my prisoner's top.
I pushed him off and ran away,
Knowing that they wouldn't stay.
Through trees, bushes, leaves and hedges,
I really needed a bowl of wedges.
Then I ran into a pond,
And the ducks were really fond,
They bit me on the toes and neck,
It felt more like a peck.
Then again it started to hail,
When I woke up, I was back in jail.

Logan Andrews (10)
Fleetdown Primary School, Dartford

We Love School

There was a girl called Cassie
She wanted a dog called Lassie
Instead, she had a cat
Who liked to wear a hat
And that was the end of that.

There was a girl named Maddy
Who was friends with a boy named Harry
They went to the park
And played with a kid called Mark
They stayed until it was dark.

There is a teacher called Miss Rehal
Who teaches us anything, we don't know how
We have fun at Fleetdown Primary
How clever are we?
When school's done on Friday, we all want to flee!

Cassie Hunt (10)
Fleetdown Primary School, Dartford

An Underwater BBQ

An underwater BBQ,
Is what we saw in Timbuktu,
The dragon licks his luscious lips,
Happily the small fish skips,
Onto a BBQ it runs,
Right onto a bright red tongue,
Splash, wade, bang, gulp,
He spits it out, it looks like pulp,
Now he pounces towards me,
I jump down a slide, "Yippee!"

I've escaped the dragon's jaws this once,
I've hidden, the dragon grunts,
An underwater BBQ,
I'll see no more in Timbuktu!

Tatyana Caffarena De Freitas (10)
Fleetdown Primary School, Dartford

Basketball

I am very good at playing basketball,
I will surely score if you give me the ball,
If you want me to score please, just give me the call,
I will make us win the game.

I play against a bear,
And I do not care,
My teammates think this match is not fair,
I don't take notice because of what's going on there,
A big, fat argument!

Kodi Nwegbu (10)
Fleetdown Primary School, Dartford

Riding The Heavy Hot Lava

I was going towards the hill of You-May-Never-Breathe.
Suddenly!
There was a loud bang!
A bright brown volcano in sight
it started as a small fire creature...

The speed of the volcano
was as fast as an eagle
swaying in the sky.

The heat was near
and I bubbled with fear.
Up and up, the fire burned
as fast as a lava rock rolling down.
Then a loud, irate popping noise
hammered down my ears.

Afterwards, another volcano was in sight.
I saw orange and red

so I was sure
that this was a volcano.

But I noticed an eruption
so I ran as fast as I could.
Luckily, I made it before the hot, flowing lava
could get a chance
to touch me.
"Thank you," I said
and I went right back home.

Kevon Stephen (8)
Haberdashers' Aske's Knights Temple Grove, Grove Park

Food Machine

I don't like beans,
But I like salad with salad cream,
I eat it so fast, I'm like a machine.
I'm on the battlefield, munching everyone,
My mouth moves so fast,
It's like bullets from a gun.
I don't like beans,
But I like my salad,
If you come to me with beans,
I will not eat like a war machine.

I like my salad with salad cream,
When I am chewing my salad,
My lips, my tongue and my teeth,
Work together like a team.

I like my salad with salad cream,
If you think salad's nasty,
You're really mean.

Now I'm going onto the beans,
They're the most disgusting thing I've ever seen.

I don't like beans,
But I like my salad with salad cream.

Zuriel Olokwei Commodore (9)
Haberdashers' Aske's Knights Temple Grove, Grove Park

Poetry Wonderland

I was in Poetry Wonderland, feeling so rad,
so I invited a long-eared elf to tea,
but he was as invisible as could be,
I didn't know where to put his teacup,
until I heard his hiccups,
I followed them, leading to a Beagle as cute as could be,
washing its puppies with water from a teacup.
As I knelt down and felt the elf's pointy ear,
I stepped back, what was that I could hear?
It was a poor dragon screaming in pain,
because he had a toothache.
I took a look in his jaw,
and what was that I saw?
A damaged cavity,
so I measured filling liquid in capacity.
Did I mention I was a vet?
Even though a dragon is not a pet,
I fixed his tooth,
and he put me on the crooked roof.

Miriam Alecsandraiaria (8)
Haberdashers' Aske's Knights Temple Grove, Grove Park

Wow

Wow, the sun
The sun is bright and has a special light
Despite its height, it beats the night
The sun never frightens those who fight
But they cannot look at its wondrous sight

Wow, the ocean
I love the ocean, it's like a nation in my imagination
I get this sensation from the sea and its decorations
Where mermaids have celebrations
And their king makes decisions.

Wow, the wind
Just where I stay, it blows me away
That's why Mother Nature made it that way
You come day by day and blow the bad things astray

The sun with its rays
Ocean with its sway
I love all and I had the chance to write about you today.

Kharis Chikezie (8)
Haberdashers' Aske's Knights Temple Grove, Grove Park

Underwater Chickens

Underwater chickens can swim underwater
Underwater chickens can fight for the fish
Underwater chickens have underwater barbecues
Underwater chickens live in the coral
Underwater chickens can swim really fast
Underwater chickens like eating chicken
Underwater chickens eat burgers
Underwater chickens have underwater barbecues with fish.

Underwater chickens have underwater races on jet skis
Underwater chickens have shoes and gloves
Chickens don't wear those things, but underwater ones do!
Underwater chickens lay water eggs
Underwater chickens can talk to fish too
Underwater chickens have underwater friends.

Rayshaughn Edwards Peddie (8)
Haberdashers' Aske's Knights Temple Grove, Grove Park

The Magical Unicorns

I cleaned my unicorn's mane very good,
I made it as sparkly as I could.
I brushed through her rainbow hair,
With stars in the air.
Whilst doing it, I drank my juice,
Then I heard a goose.
I suddenly got a text,
I knew what was going to happen next.
Magically, a new unicorn appeared,
And that was very weird.
With the moon in the sky,
I started to cry.
This was happening on land,
And the unicorn was in a band.
Next to me appeared fairy dust,
And a box covered in rust.
I made a cake,
But I ached.
The unicorn disappeared,
Inside, I cheered,
Then happily enjoyed the cake.

Daisy Hargreaves (8)
Haberdashers' Aske's Knights Temple Grove, Grove Park

Dancing With A Cloud

Can you imagine what dancing with a cloud feels like?
It must feel so fluffy
with the air clashing against your face,
I bet it smells like sweet pink candyfloss.
The cloud is as soft as a pillow
and as light as a feather.
I wonder if some clouds dance?
Maybe they do hip hop and ballet
but don't forget jazz.
Some clouds move across the sky
elegantly as a swam
and as fast as a cheetah dancing hip hop.
When I dance with the clouds
I feel delightful
and like I'm on top of the world.
I feel loved and lost in time.

Naoma Diop-Morgan (9)
Haberdashers' Aske's Knights Temple Grove, Grove Park

My Adventure In Space

I went to a tea party in space,
I took part in an alien race,
To my surprise, I came first place,
The green alien got angry and gave me a chase,
He tripped over his silky shoelace,
Slowly, he skidded on his face,
Ended up with a gigantic graze,
He screamed with a craze,
My beady eyes thought, *oh my days!*
He popped open his brown briefcase,
Out shot Aunty Grace,
With a big fat grin on her face,
Startled, I panicked and vanished,
Doing zigzags in outer space.

Priya Blackwood (8)
Haberdashers' Aske's Knights Temple Grove, Grove Park

Greg's Gigantic Adventure

Banging and crashing like thunder,
Gigantic footsteps are following mine,
Hopping and stomping to keep up in time.
All of a sudden, a giant octopus appears from behind my ears,
"Oi!" he shouts. "Get in the line, you're wasting my time!"

I take a look up, what do I see?
A horrendous giant looking down at me!
Standing and shaking and wanting to run
The giant replies, "Let's have some fun."
So we play hopscotch under the scorching sun.

Owen Robert Thomas Lynch (8)
Haberdashers' Aske's Knights Temple Grove, Grove Park

Crazy Cat

My cat gives me a headache
She was sad
But I was mad
She scratched the door
She's a pain in the neck
"What the heck?"
Miaow, miaow, screaming all the way
I bought her a new tray
What a crazy cat.

What a crazy cat
Who sat on a mat
She loves to chase a rat
She's very unique
Like a boutique
She's hairy, furry and fluffy
I put her in a cage
It makes her rage
What a crazy cat.

Xantia-Reay Destiny Wright (8)
Haberdashers' Aske's Knights Temple Grove, Grove Park

Lick A Shark

The other day, I licked a shark
It was in the daytime, so it wasn't dark.
Slippery and wet, the shark was grey
Have I already said that it was in the day?
My tongue felt cold, the shark was slimy
If I told my grandad, he'd say "Cor blimey!
Fancy licking a shark!" he'd say
"Was it at night or in the day?"
"It was in the day," I would say with glee
"I licked the shark before it licked me!"

Alyza Foster Baker (8)
Haberdashers' Aske's Knights Temple Grove, Grove Park

The Dragon As A Pet

Big googly eyes,
A big green back,
Spikes on his head,
Ugly yellow teeth,
The dragon as a pet.

It doesn't speak,
Always eats,
Can't fly,
It can drink,
The dragon as a pet.

Its mummy left it when it was four,
His mum's name is Law,
His dad's name is Drew,
The pet as a dragon.

He loves Mr Lion,
They get on very well,
They like lemonade,
The pet as a dragon.

Alfie Dolby (8)
Haberdashers' Aske's Knights Temple Grove, Grove Park

The Magic Hole

I woke up in my bed
I looked round slowly
I saw a magical swirl on the floor
it swallowed me up
it took me through time...

I opened my eyes
to see a surprise
it was a world of adventure!
I saw a baby dragon
I was about to touch the dragon
but then came lots of gnomes...

I ran into the hole
I woke myself
I opened my eyes
and I got dressed
and had a lovely day.

Alfie Jay Richie Hurstwaite (8)
Haberdashers' Aske's Knights Temple Grove, Grove Park

Saw A Mermaid At A Beach

I went to the beach
wide and blue ocean
went to sit on a beach chair
saw something strange in the lovely water
I wondered what it was
"Huh, it's a mermaid!"
She was more magical than a fairy
a unicorn, a dragon or a princess
she turned me into a pretty little mermaid
my tail was amazing, beautiful
now I had a majestic, beautiful tail
or was it just a big dream...?

Isabella Casarin De Almeida (8)
Haberdashers' Aske's Knights Temple Grove, Grove Park

Happy Holidays

Holidays are happy days
Holidays are sweet days
On holidays, you can have meat days
Sunbeds are cool
They're near the pool
After you go to the bar
At the pool
Always play with a ball
I hang out with my dad, he's so cool
We go on the slide and fall into the pool
I love my mum
We have so much fun
Watching the shows and eating popcorn
Holidays are happy days.

Javeed Omar Grant (8)
Haberdashers' Aske's Knights Temple Grove, Grove Park

Halloween Night

With a chatter of teeth
And a shiver down my spine
Our buckets filled with sweets
And the door shut and whined.
As we rang the bell
A shiver went down my spine
As a grunt hissed
Then a slam awoke a freak
Which sent us all running
As fangs pierced my skin
I felt drowsy
I passed out like a deer in the wilderness
When I woke up in the dirt
I heard a twig snap...

Millie Louise Briley (8)
Haberdashers' Aske's Knights Temple Grove, Grove Park

Flying Fish

There are all sorts of fantastic fish
like a clownfish, a whale and others.
Fish don't mean any harm, don't eat them
they're my buddies and can be yours as well.
They watch football just like you
you could be a vegetarian.
They have wonderful properties like you
don't eat them, please.

Daniel Burnham (8)
Haberdashers' Aske's Knights Temple Grove, Grove Park

My Pet Lion

I was sitting here, stroking my lion,
He had very soft fur.
He started to growl,
He had a little cat's purr,
He had a very loud howl,
Everyone would call him a her.

Harvey Ward (8)
Haberdashers' Aske's Knights Temple Grove, Grove Park

A Mystery Hole

As I was feeling bored, I went to explore,
I saw nothing except a hole in the floor.
Keen to see what was inside,
I saw a hole very wide.
As I jumped inside,
I realised I was trapped inside!
When I walked forward,
I saw a mysterious passage.
Argh, the mystery place was hell.
I saw a million holes ahead of me,
I leapt into the first hole and saw Candyland!
Now this is not hell,
In fact it's heaven.
I thought of licking a candy giant...
"Bye, sweet Candyland,"
I say as I climb up a blue candyfloss ladder.
Wait, I went through the wrong hole
Because now I've turned into a fairy feeding a baby unicorn!

Soon I realise you need to get through all the holes
Then I realise I am stuck again...
Oh no!

Sunni Li-Hutchins (7)
High Firs Primary School, Swanley

Candy Land

I fell through a doorway and felt kind of dizzy,
When I woke up I thought I was in Candy
Wonderland!
Gummy birds and chocolate houses,
Much more exciting places.
Several lollipop trees,
Honeybees,
It feels like candy heaven!
The place I like the look of
Is the shop made out of doughnuts.
So many places,
So many custard waterfalls!
Everything looks so tasty.
I personally have a question -
Would it all melt?
I am going to visit the crisp factory,
Which is supposed to look so beautiful and crispy.
Apparently there are 10,200 sprinkles there as well.
If you want to visit, fall through a doorway
But make sure you don't go to Candy Hospital.

The day I fell in the doorway
Is a day I won't forget.

Eliza Grace Robertson-Willmot (7)
High Firs Primary School, Swanley

Lola And The Dragon

Lola bought a cat from the market place
She had a crazy idea of them going to space.
The cat was magic and began to talk
Lola listens to his voice when they walk.
It turned into night and they followed the moon
As they entered the forest they heard a tune.
Lola's face turned from happy to sad
Something happened they thought was bad...
A dragon appeared, looking scary!
They wondered why he was hairy.
The dragon was friendly, cuddly and kind
Lola and the cat changed their minds.
Lola asked, "Will you fly us up there?"
The dragon replied, "Yes, hold onto my hair."
They flew off into the sky, up to the moon
When they landed they had a piece of cake with a spoon!

Chiana Lei Webb (8)
High Firs Primary School, Swanley

I'd Rather Be Me

Oops, I have shrunk,
Shrunk to the size of an ant!
I wish I knew where I went.
The sky is still blue,
The grass is still green,
But I'm the size of a tiny baked bean!
Everything is so tall and I am so small,
I wonder if ants have any fun at all!
Quick, quick, somebody is coming,
I can hear them humming.
Run, run, as fast as you can,
I'm definitely not as quick as the gingerbread man!
Hiding in the bush, hearing the world so much
louder than before,
I don't want to be this small anymore.
Bugs must be so smart,
Their world is miles apart.
I can't wait until I grow again,
I'd prefer being me again!

Nicole Jade King (8)
High Firs Primary School, Swanley

The Mysterious Doors

When I'm about to perform,
I suddenly feel quite warm.
Then I turn around and see,
A mysterious door in front of me.
The door opens and I step inside,
And find something by my side...
It is a fairy,
She is looking ever so merry.
Then she tells me to go through another door,
So now I am in a book store.
Then there's chanting, the books are saying, "Read me, Read me..."
The noise is ear-splitting, it sounds like a crashing sea.
Then a door appears,
And I give away a few tears.
I jump through it,
And I'm in my ballet kit.
Then I dance,
Time has not given a glance.

Jalena Li-Hutchins (10)
High Firs Primary School, Swanley

The Wizard's Phoenix

In I crept one hot summer's night,
To the wizard's chamber full of delights.
Across the room, there was such a sight,
A blazing phoenix lighting up the night!
As he burned, I watched on in fright
And all at once, the blaze grew bright!
Then suddenly, all was as dark as night,
And a cry could be heard from deep inside.
Further in I crept that night,
To see inside the cage a most amazing sight...
A baby phoenix rising up from the ashes,
Bringing a new life full of astonishing light!
Back out I crept, into the dark of midnight,
The rising of the phoenix was my day's highlight.

Jack Morris (8)
High Firs Primary School, Swanley

Volcano Surf!

"I want to ride some lava," said little Fred
"No," said Fred's mum, her head full of dread.
"Go to bed now, time for you to dream."
"Oh," said Fred, his mum's a drama queen!
In the dead of night he went to catch some waves
"Should I, Teddy Turtle?" He nodded his head and dreamed.
As soon as he got outside, what did he see?
"It's beautiful!" he said in his dream.
He hopped on his board and surfed at terrific speed.
Half an hour later, he woke up from his dream
And saw Teddy Turtle staring at him...
"Huh?"

Harry Robert Loftus (8)
High Firs Primary School, Swanley

My Friend, Bob

My friend, Bob, is coming for his holiday
I wonder how long he will stay?
I have waited all morning but here he comes now
Where will he land? Watch out for the cow!

There is something you should know about Bob
He is an alien who comes from the planet Boblob.
Bob is purple with ten eyes and four ears
You would never guess he's been alive 362 years.

We have cabbage soup for lunch which Bob really likes
Maybe this afternoon we can go fly on our hoverbikes.
I always have the best time with my friend Bob
Maybe one day I can go visit him on Planet Boblob.

Francesca Valentino (9)
High Firs Primary School, Swanley

Treasure Hunt

I found a map,
When my dad was having a nap.
The map told us to go to an island,
I thought it was Thailand.
I woke my dad,
Then he got his iPad,
It said to go to Mars!
I couldn't see anything in the sky except for stars.
There was one rocket,
Like the one my dad had in his pocket.
When I shot up in the sky on the rocket,
I saw the planet!
There was treasure on Mars,
And I could easily see a box of tarts.

Veda Trivedi (7)
High Firs Primary School, Swanley

Secret Agents

August 19th 1963
We had a mission, my agents and me.
There was no doubt about it, it would be tricky,
So my agents and me called for Micky.
Micky the dog, he helps us a lot,
But when he was a puppy he slept in a cot... Err!
So we went off to do our mission,
There were three paths, all were partitioned.
We didn't know where to go
So we ran down the middle one and went with the flow...

Olivia Webb (10)
High Firs Primary School, Swanley

Me And My Dragon

I have a pet dragon, his name is Rob
His favourite food is corn on the cob.
He likes to play hide-and-seek,
But when I hide I'm sure he peeps.
He plays with me in the bath
And does fun things to make me laugh.
When we go out, people like to stare
But I love him so much I really don't care.

Lucy Baylis (8)
High Firs Primary School, Swanley

The Avengers

The Avengers are an unstoppable team,
They fit together just like a dream.
These five can stop anyone that gets in their way,
They can stop bad guys in less than a day.
The Avengers go to the Avengers' tower to learn their skill
The Avengers always get their kill.

Harry Tampion (8)
High Firs Primary School, Swanley

Cookie Monster

I took a path along the thorns and brambles,
Following the cookie shambles.
It was a cookie monster,
It was just a youngster,
And it needed its 100 cookies a day.
So I tapped on its back
And got ready to make its day,
I gave him some cookies!

Yuri Ayukegba (10)
High Firs Primary School, Swanley

Reptiles, Oh Reptiles

Reptiles, oh reptiles
They're one of a kind
From slithering snakes to angry alligators
Lizards and turtles,
King cobras, boas and adders
Stay away from Komodo dragons
Be ready to run
Hiding where no one knows...

Megan (10)
High Firs Primary School, Swanley

Teddy And Me

I bought a teddy called Teddy Bee
He is yellow and smarter than me
Every night he wakes up from his bed
And both of us go on adventures instead
I'd give anything to see him,
I love my teddy.

James William Loftus (8)
High Firs Primary School, Swanley

Roblox

A land of rocks
Made from blocks,
And 10,000 games
Some with red flames.
Play with friends
And on cliff bends,
So much fun
It's like iced buns!

Matthew Collett (8)
High Firs Primary School, Swanley

Lilly Maci

In a normal world
There are no stories to tell
No endings to end
And no sweets that fall from the sky.
No dragons that love you or care
Not even a little old bear
So fall down the rabbit hole
Into Poetry Land
And see what you could come back up for.
In Poetry Land there are stories to tell
And endings to end
And sweets that fall from the sky.
There's a dragon who's a pet for Lilly Maci
And a pointy-hatted wizard with his beard stuck in a tree.
But good Lilly Maci is a friendly little girl
Who loves her own little life
So, "Thank you," she says, and back she goes to the normal world
Where there are no stories to tell

And no endings to read.
So, goodbye, lovely Lilly Maci.

Zara Page (9)
Hilden Grange School, Tonbridge

Outer Space Penguin

There once was a penguin called Joe
He was very small and low
He visited a different land
It had a big pile of sand
He saw food, it was food land
You could eat anything there with your hands
How delicious! It was fun
It was good and in the sun.

Sharna Louise Cole (7)
Kings Hill School, Kings Hill

My Trip To The Beach With Rory

My dragon is called Rory,
He always likes to tell a story...
We went to the beach,
He ate a juicy peach.
He has big, stony feet,
And he loves to eat, eat, eat!
Rory's tail is very swishy,
That makes his toenails go all mushy.

Eliza Toby (8)
Kings Hill School, Kings Hill

The Knight And The Monster

There once was a knight who loved to fight.
He met a monster as red as a lobster.
The monster began to pull down trees that were full of bees.
He loved eating wood, he saw Robin Hood,
Who was holding a book about a cook!

Zoë Davies Rean (7)
Kings Hill School, Kings Hill

Terrapin Glow

Terrapins, terrapins everywhere,
They glow so much, it makes them easier to clutch!
I love to see their peeking heads,
When they're in their beds,
I love the way their eyes goggle,
It makes my brain boggle!

Rory Clayton (7)
Kings Hill School, Kings Hill

Riding A Lightning Bolt

My feet are crackling and my hands are popping,
My body is jumping and my tummy is fizzing,
The electricity is whizzing and I am jumping around,
Then I crash and I hit the ground.

Asad Siddiqui (7)
Kings Hill School, Kings Hill

Peter The Cheetah

There once was a cheetah called Peter
Peter was heating his meat on a heater
He sat on a wooden seat
Waiting for his meat to heat.

Washington Brouet (7)
Kings Hill School, Kings Hill

The Noises From The Library

In the library, it was eerily quiet,
It wasn't really a place you'd expect a riot.
I crept inside and shut the door,
All of a sudden, books fell to the floor.
The quietness was instantly broken,
The thousands of books were all awoken,
By the big heavy storybook,
With dusty leaves that shook and shook.
A voice boomed out of the flimsy pages,
A sound that hadn't been heard for ages.
"Come on, come on, it's time to party,
There's no time for this malarky."
The books got up, shook and had a wiggle,
Then they let out a mighty giggle.
Books were running back and forth,
All directions, south, east, west and north.
Their giggles soon turned to chatter,
I even thought I heard the Mad Hatter!

The noise in the library was so unreal,
I could do nothing but stand open-mouthed and stock still.
I tried to engage Tom Thumb in a chat,
Only to be attacked by a Hogwarts bat.
Alice from Wonderland said, "Oh, do come for tea."
Then I got stung by Pooh Bear's honeybee.
I turned towards the door,
But was thrown to the floor.
The three little pigs opened it wide,
Meaning the big bad wolf had rushed outside.
At this moment, I needed to flee,
The excitement meant I needed a wee!
Out of the door I went in a rush,
The noise in the library becoming a hush.
Once outside the room, I stopped and said,
"That was enough to wake Sleeping Beauty from her bed!"

Gemma May Binder (10)

Selling CE Primary School, Selling

My Next-Door Neighbour's A Witch

My next-door neighbour's definitely a witch,
At Cackle Drive, number six,
Haunting the narrow street,
Silence like snow whenever she speaks,
She has an ugly wart on the end of her nose,
And long, pointy boots that cover her toes,
My mother told me to keep away,
Or her cat might mistake me for prey,
She likes to go out at night,
With her tall black hat slanted to the right,
Her teeth are green and rotten,
And her coal-black cape is made of cotton,
I expect she travels around on her broom,
Because how else would she get over traffic so soon?
She loves wearing black, rather like a goth,
And her favourite animals are toads, rats, cats and moths,
Her voice is a high-pitched shriek,
Also, her hair is black and bleak,

But, one day, she wasn't at home,
Not a sign of her, just her broken gnomes,
The police were looking 'til noon,
But I expect she probably rode off towards the moon.

Evie Vincent (10)

Selling CE Primary School, Selling

Wintry Treats

I woke up this morning, jumped out of bed,
Pulled open the curtains and slapped my head.

Snow fell gently to the ground,
But they were marshmallows, fluffy and round.

I opened my window to have some to eat,
All fluffy and sweet, this surely was a treat!

Icicles were hanging on the side of the house,
They were sweet candy canes being licked by a mouse.

The leaves and the branches were glittering bright,
Dusted with icing sugar, sparkly white.

I rushed outside to get me a lick,
But something stopped me from being so quick.

Just then, I realised it was all a dream,
And my fantasy world was not what it seemed.

Megan Page (10)
Selling CE Primary School, Selling

Family And Friends

F un is all we need
A nd love is what we come for.
M ums and dads are the ones that will love you.
I love my family and friends.
L ove one another.
Y ou can love yourself

A nd be yourself.
N ever give up.
D are to be different.

F riends and family keep you safe.
R eal life is a place for all of us.
I must love everyone.
E veryone will be your friend.
N o one should be lonely.
D o you love one another?
S ee what you can see.

Ella Denton (10)
Selling CE Primary School, Selling

Magnificent Creatures

Enchanters, however hard they try,
Will always be wondrous.
Now, extraordinary is just the thing,
To get me wondering if enchanters are marvellous.

I cannot help but stop and look at mythical mermaids.
Down, down, down into the darkness of the mermaids.
Gently, they go - the mythologic, the unreal, the mythological.

When I think of pixies, I see a little person.
Down, down, down into the darkness of the pixies.
Gently they go - the addled, the hirsute, the woolly-minded.

Kelsie Jayes (10)
Selling CE Primary School, Selling

Fishing Catastrophe!

I was fishing off an old dusty rock,
And my hook caught on a mouldy sock!
I held out my rod for attempt number two,
Splashed out of the water and out came a shoe.
A shoal of fish went swimming past,
I had to put the line in, and fast.
I reached into my basket to grab some bait,
Unfortunately, I was much too late.
All eight fish went swimming past,
But I had caught something (at last).
I reeled it in with excitement and joy,
To the disappointment of finding a stuffed toy!

Freya Elizabeth Mogford (11)
Selling CE Primary School, Selling

Was I Going To Live Through The Day?

I went on a holiday that went very wrong,
We sat by the campfire and sang a song.
All of a sudden, it went pitch-black,
"What's going on?" Mum shouted back.

The clouds grew darker,
The wind began to howl.
The tent blew away,
So did the towel.

The fire went out,
The car rolled away.
No one was about,
Was I going to live through the day...?

Marianne Harris (10)
Selling CE Primary School, Selling

The Storm

The wind picked up,
As the rain came down,
The thunder began,
The sky's clouds thickened,
The sky grew darker,
You could hear the tapping,
As the rain came down,
Onto the windowpane,
There were flashes of light,
That gave me a fright,
As the rain came down,
My sister was scared,
I went up the stairs,
I felt like nobody cared.

Harriet Deal (10)
Selling CE Primary School, Selling

Get Up And Go Gorilla

Boom, boom, boom on his chest,
The cheeky gorilla called his friends and guests,
Swinging from tree to tree, he jumped into an Addison Lee.
"Taximan, taximan, I love your fake tan,
I've stolen your cab, catch me if you can!"
Off he drove with the driver in pursuit,
Only then did they realise it was a thief in a gorilla suit!

Brooke Sophia Childs (10)
Selling CE Primary School, Selling

Perky Pets

In the living room, on the mat,
Is Old Mog's hairy habitat.

Squeaking loudly, waiting for food,
Guineas, are you in a bad mood?

Sweeping her paw under the door,
Mog wants a cuddle, that's for sure.

The latest arrival's a bundle of fun,
All day and night, he wishes to run.

Sammy James Wright (11)
Selling CE Primary School, Selling

My Little Christmas Tree

One little angel
Sitting on my tree.

Two large presents
Hidden there for me.

Three red beads
Wrapped around my tree.

Four coloured lights
Shining all around me.

Five swinging baubles
Glowing brightly.

Oh, what a lovely sight
For us all to see!

Matthew Thomson (11)
Selling CE Primary School, Selling

My Tree Friends

My friend Steve is a friend with whom I talk,
Although he was a tree, *strange*, I thought,
Before, he had told me about his rooty leg,
So then we pulled him out with clothes pegs!
"I am free," he said as he climbed out,
Then he was free and danced all about!

Wyatt Richard Harman (10)
Selling CE Primary School, Selling

Dinner On A Cloud!

I'm inviting my friends to dinner
But we both need to get a bit thinner.
No chips or chocolate will be on the menu,
But my friend, he says, "Reconsider the venue."
He is afraid of heights and doesn't eat meat,
So we are going to a town for a place to eat!

Theo Butler (11)
Selling CE Primary School, Selling

The Autumn Days

A utumn brings a chill to the air
U mbrellas keep you dry, but can make you fly
T he leaves turn colourful
U nderfoot, the leaves go *crunch*
M any people jump into piles of leaves
N ot a sound is heard in the autumn mist.

Alice Regan-Adams (10)
Selling CE Primary School, Selling

Over The Rainbow

Over the rainbow,
You will see,
A pot of gold,
Gleaming free,
Unicorns dance,
Mermaids sing,
It never ends,
It's an unforgettable dream.

Ellie Annique Pynn (11)
Selling CE Primary School, Selling

Cat Ears Curious

C ats are more into cat ears than us
A nts do not have cat ears!
T ime can have cat ears.

E at cat ears
A nd they can be in different styles
R ing the cat ears because you can be best friends
S trong with them - there are muscles in them.

Meliesa Ates (10)
Small Haven Independent Special Needs School, Ramsgate

Lovely Mermaids

M ermaids are beautiful
E arrings are beautiful and
R eally pink
M ermaids are magical
A nd friends of the fish!
I love mermaids
D id you know they wear seashells in their hair?
S hells are made into necklaces.

Poppy Scutt (10)
Small Haven Independent Special Needs School, Ramsgate

Dancing Fish

D ancing fish are like
A crobats
N o one
C an stop them
I t's impossible
N ice to watch
G ood fish.

F ast as a flash
I n the air
S pinning
H appily.

James Akhurst (9)
Small Haven Independent Special Needs School, Ramsgate

Tiger

T igers are stripy and scary!
I love tigers, they are soft.
"G rr!" say the tigers.
"E at me," says the magical fairy.
"R eally? Do you want to eat me?"

Kimarley Maragh-West (9)
Small Haven Independent Special Needs School, Ramsgate

Flying Fish

F ish can fly,
L eaping into the air,
Y elling really loudly.

F ire-breathing,
I mpossible to catch,
S parkling in the sky,
H ear them clap their fins.

Emily Fitzgerald (10)
Small Haven Independent Special Needs School, Ramsgate

Pool Party On Venus

One night I lay in bed, I just couldn't get to sleep,
I shoved and turned, wiggled and jiggled, I gave up counting sheep.
Then suddenly I saw a key to a shiny golden door,
I got out of bed and unlocked it, where would I explore?
When I landed there was a lot of fuss!
I had really arrived on Planet Venus!
But it wasn't burning, hot or rocky,
An exciting, crazy pool party - that's all I could see
Aliens cried in a water slide - even I had a go or two.
I looked around, there was no ground but always something to do
Creatures surfed and snacks would float,
There was even a Martian on a sailing boat!
Spotty creatures lived in underwater trees,
There was no such thing as striped bumblebees!
There were unicorn-dolphins called uniphins,
Oh they do sound lovely when they sing!
The stars shone high throughout the sky,
Some aliens could even fly.

But then I had to leave - I didn't want to go,
This place was really busy though!
So then I landed on my bed,
No longer needing to rest my head.

Nyah Willow Martin (8)
Snodland CE Primary School, Snodland

The Cool School Poem

It's a dream to meet the Queen before my teens
And have biscuits and tea.
She will be wearing a crown
And I will wear a hat that is supreme
Looking like a McFlurry ice cream.
I walk around the palace
And feel like I'm in Wonderland like Alice.
I wish I could perform to the Queen
By winning Britain's Got Talent
It would be lights, camera and action
With a crowd with a good reaction
I made my hat with satisfaction.
As the hat sits on my head
I can hear the sea
And almost see stars
In broad daylight appearing.
I'll find the biggest cookie I can find
And I will share it because I'm kind
If they wanted to hear this again
I would give them a rewind.

Evelyn Jean Open (10)
Snodland CE Primary School, Snodland

Gross Unicorns

If unicorns existed in the real world today,
We would scream and shout and say, "Hooray!"
But are these creatures as beautiful as they seem,
Or are they gross and not like the dream?
Is there a truth we have not been told?
What about the lies that we have been sold?
The real unicorn you will soon find out
Is not what you'd expect to find out about...
She smells like rubbish and not like rainbows,
She has messy hair and never wears bows.
She is not as kind or soft as she would look,
She'd stomp all over your homework book!
So don't be fooled by this tricky pest,
They're one of a kind and not like the rest.

Danielle Durey (8)
St James' CE Primary Academy, Isle Of Grain

The Darkness Wonderland

As I slowly crept into the dragon's cave,
In front of me was a grave.
I walked in a bit further past the grave,
I also saw a cape and a dark cake.
What shall I do,
Shall I smash it?
Shall I leave it,
Or shall I eat it?
Am I dreaming?
I don't know!
Then I saw a dragon black and white
What shall I do?
Shall I wake it,
Shall I give it a fright?
I felt the really scaly dragon...

Evie Hood (8)
St James' CE Primary Academy, Isle Of Grain

The Tale Of Cheshire Cat

The Cheshire Cat fell from the sky
It was raining popcorn from way up high.

As we were walking on the land
We saw a big brass band.

Could I hear someone screaming?
Was this real or was I dreaming?

The cat sat on the mug of coffee,
He purred and said, "It tastes like toffee."

Oh how I wish I was riding a unicorn
Distracted again, he smelled some popcorn.

He smelled it down the rabbit hole
Where has he gone? Maybe to see the mole...

Emily Grant (8)
St James' CE Primary Academy, Isle Of Grain

The Tale Of Mermaid 1/2 Unicorn

As I stepped into the mirror,
I saw a flowing river

In the river were fluffy pink unicorns,
Eating some delicious popcorn

I don't want these animals to depart,
Unicorns have a lovely heart

I like seeing the lovely rainbows,
JoJo has a dog called Bobo

The unicorns also like eating cupcakes,
Here I even have a pet snake!

My name is called Lollipop 'cause it's a girl,
I also have a jewel which looks like a pearl.

Megan Giles (7)
St James' CE Primary Academy, Isle Of Grain

The Island

As I slowly stepped in the moly hole,
I saw Santa at the North Pole!

I drank toffee,
I smelled coffee.

Santa was there,
Now he's gone but where?

As I walked on the land,
I saw a big band.

The Cheshire Cat fell from the sky,
With raining popcorn way up high.

I saw a monster with bright green eyes,
Licking his lips for flies.

I had something on my feet,
It tasted like a bit of meat...

Riley Skinner (7)
St James' CE Primary Academy, Isle Of Grain

Magical Cave

As I quickly stepped into a dark cave
Was I feeling scared? Was I feeling brave?
A fluffy bunny jumped from up high
It started to fly then ate a pie.
It started laughing
But then I heard something startling...
I saw a big slimy snail
It smelled like a big fat whale.
I touched the white rabbit
That was playing with a tablet
What a crazy day I've had
At least it wasn't school, that would be bad!

Jessica Hood (7)
St James' CE Primary Academy, Isle Of Grain

An Adventure To Wonderland

As I stepped into the dark dragon cave,
Was I feeling afraid, was I feeling brave?

In the cave
I saw a grave.

I heard a dragon
Go by with a wagon,
I saw a parrot with a talent
And it had a bump
A big thump.

I did taste
A lace
In the bath
That was in a park.

I touched the parrot
With the lovely talent
And another parrot thumped
With a bump.

Freddie Williams (7)
St James' CE Primary Academy, Isle Of Grain

Candy Cats And Bubblegum Vans

A candy cat palace,
And lots of mallets.

The palace was gold,
And very, very bold.

Lots of bubbles popping
And engines rocking.

Smelling lollipops,
And choccy rocks.

Eating choc 'n' lollipops,
Bubblegum in my mouth pops.

Feeling bubbles alike,
Candy corns are what I like!

Be careful where you go,
You might get tied in a fondant bow!

Esther Gurr (7)
St James' CE Primary Academy, Isle Of Grain

The Crazy Island

I slowly stepped into the monster cave
I saw something creepy, it was a grave.

In my dream
I saw a beam.

I smelled toffee
In my coffee.

I saw a black cat
In my hat.

I saw a dragon
In a wagon.

I saw a monster with bright green eyes
Licking his lips for big flies!

I had something on my feet
It tasted like a bit of meat...

Joshua Lee (7)
St James' CE Primary Academy, Isle Of Grain

The Beardasa Runs

As I stepped into the gloomy desert
In a cave there was a grave
I couldn't fight, I saw a light
In the grave.
I saw a stone
It was a giant stone
In a dish there was a fish
I looked around and heard a sound
The fish was on the boil but it was a mess.
I felt a little stress with the mess!
I heard a bless you coming from my chest
But it soon went away like the rest.

Tyler Stewart (7)
St James' CE Primary Academy, Isle Of Grain

Sweets And Dragons

In a kingdom of sweets and dragons,
I saw a beast riding a wagon.
Then I touched the dragon's cookie tail,
It felt crispy like a piece of mail.
I heard a sweet,
Dancing to the beat,
I smelt the sugar,
Boiling on the cooker.
The sweet melted in my belly,
It's more fun to eat them than watching telly.
Now it's the end,
Do go back and tell a friend!

Jasper Paul Winder (7)
St James' CE Primary Academy, Isle Of Grain

Wonder Candyland

I walked through the gate
Then I saw my favourite mate.

I saw a pretty mole
In a very pretty hole.

I was drinking my coffee
It smelled like toffee.

I saw a pig
In a wig!

I saw a beard
That was very weird.

I needed to mend
My best friend.

There was something on my feet
It tasted a bit like fresh meat...

Lily Owens (7)
St James' CE Primary Academy, Isle Of Grain

Floating Chickens

Floating chickens in the air,
Are usually so unfair.

They are not right,
And do get in a fight.

Always fighting for their lives,
But who would survive?

When they are nice,
They are soft like rice.

After they were sad,
They were extremely mad.

Do not come too close,
Or you might come back as roast!

Isaac Stephen Hirshler (7)
St James' CE Primary Academy, Isle Of Grain

The Cute Baby

Am I hearing a terrible scream
Or am I asleep, inside a dream?
The dragon looked after the cute baby knight,
Hold on a minute, this dream doesn't seem right!
The baby is crying a terrible sound,
Throughout the cave it echoes around.
The dragon soothes him, blowing smoke from his nose
The baby knight giggles as it tickles his toes.

Sienna Amber Neilson (7)
St James' CE Primary Academy, Isle Of Grain

Wonderland

When I went out of the house,
I saw a giant, stinky, fat mouse.
I went further down the road,
I saw a giant toad.
I heard Santa race,
On the way to a jaguar base.
I saw a snake,
It was made out of cake.
I saw something red,
It was a monster bed.
I saw a chimpanzee,
It was doing karate!

Max Strickland (7)
St James' CE Primary Academy, Isle Of Grain

A Goat On The Boat

I was flying on a goat,
The goat landed on a boat.
Did the boat need a coat?
Through the cold it did float.
For breakfast I had oats on the goat!
Today I wanted to have a vote,
About the moat that goes around the castle of the goat.
I wrote a poem on the boat,
But then what happened to the goat?

Scarlett Abel (7)
St James' CE Primary Academy, Isle Of Grain

Drawbridge

D oes a good job
R eally strong
A rrows can't shoot in
W ater underneath
B ridge
R ight in front of the castle
I t is strong
D rawn up by
G reat chains
E nemies don't go into the castle.

Ruby Elizabeth Carter (5)
St James' CE Primary Academy, Isle Of Grain

Volcano Pony

I went to a volcano
I travelled on a train - oh!
I saw a silver unicorn
Covered in glitter with a horn
As I came close, she ran away
Over the hills and far away
The smell of ash was in the air
A barbecued sausage was going spare.

Lily Hill (7)
St James' CE Primary Academy, Isle Of Grain

Jester

J olly and strange
E xcited and interesting
S trong arms and a tiny brain
T errified of upsetting the king
E nthusiastic and funny because he eats too much sugar
R estless at the end of the day.

Gracie Beeching (7)
St James' CE Primary Academy, Isle Of Grain

Knight

K ings and queens make knights look after them
N eed to be careful
I n the castle they are kept safe
G uards the castle
H airy dragons exploding
T all tower, it's bigger than the knight.

Daisy Stratford (6)
St James' CE Primary Academy, Isle Of Grain

Jester

J olly and really silly
E xciting and fun to make the queen laugh
S illy and strange
T oo silly for telling silly jokes
E verybody laughs at the silly jester
R eally funny and silly.

Ella Hulbert (6)
St James' CE Primary Academy, Isle Of Grain

Silly Dog

The dog ran across the road with his poo.
The dogs are so fluffy like rabbits.
A person took a dog called Mogg,
The dog was zooming across the road.
He bumped his head on the pole,
Bark, bark, bark, bark!

Lola Page (7)
St James' CE Primary Academy, Isle Of Grain

Lands

Unicorns are on the sweet sands,
and dry lands.

A talking ice cream came out of nowhere,
"Help!" I shouted. Does nobody care?

Purple llamas in the orange lake,
am I dreaming or am I awake?

Freya Pucknell-Watts (7)
St James' CE Primary Academy, Isle Of Grain

Knight

K eep safe with your armour
N eed to keep on training
I ndestructible sword
G rab your armour and fight
H ave your armour to keep safe
T ake the sword to help you fight.

Harrison George Wright (6)
St James' CE Primary Academy, Isle Of Grain

Knight

K nights are tough and powerful
N aughty and spiteful
I n the castle where they live
G reat and
H igh and mighty
T he knight has a shiny shield.

Logan James Almeida-Brown (6)
St James' CE Primary Academy, Isle Of Grain

King

K ings are hard and they are special
I gnores the queen because she doesn't want to go
N aughty because he is bossy to servants
G reedy at dinner and breakfast.

Milly Suleyman (6)
St James' CE Primary Academy, Isle Of Grain

Knight

K eep enemies out
N ice armour
I t rides on horses
G reat shiny armour
H elmets to protect their head
T hey shoot out of arrow slits.

Chloe Nelson (6)
St James' CE Primary Academy, Isle Of Grain

Jester

J olly and happy
E xciting
S trange and jolly
T errified of upsetting the king and queen
E verybody laughing
R unning in the castle.

Lois Miller (6)
St James' CE Primary Academy, Isle Of Grain

Jester

J olly, funny clowns
E xcited about jokes
S illy and strange
T oo hyper from jokes
E ntertaining the king and queen
R eally clever.

Lloyd AJ Wilkinson (7)
St James' CE Primary Academy, Isle Of Grain

Knight

K eep the castle safe
N eed to be quiet
I nside the castle
G et rid of the baddies
H elmets for their heads
T hey ride on horses.

Kara Kinslow (5)
St James' CE Primary Academy, Isle Of Grain

Drawbridge

Drawn up by chains
River underneath
Arrow slits
Water
Bridge goes up
Royals kept safe
It keeps enemies out
Does a good job
Enemies can't get in!

Amelia Francesca Siggers (5)
St James' CE Primary Academy, Isle Of Grain

Knight

K eeps enemies out
N ice and strong
I t rides on horses
G reat shiny armour
H elmets to protect their heads
T hey are mighty.

Melanie Elena Sutton (5)
St James' CE Primary Academy, Isle Of Grain

Knight

K eeps the castle safe
N eed to be quiet
I n the castle
G ets rid of baddies
H elmets
T hey like to wear armour.

Theodore Joseph Stillings (5)
St James' CE Primary Academy, Isle Of Grain

Queen

Q ueens are very bossy
U nkind because she locks people up
E verybody likes her
E very queen has a crown
N ice and strong.

Hollie Anne Hawksworth (6)
St James' CE Primary Academy, Isle Of Grain

Knight

K eep the castle safe
N eed to be quiet
I nside the castle
G et rid of the baddies
H elmets
T hey wear armour.

Charlie Jenson Dominic Wright (5)
St James' CE Primary Academy, Isle Of Grain

Knight

K eep safe wearing armour
N ice and strong
I n the castle
G reat armour
H elmets
T hey guard the castle.

Harrison Keir (5)
St James' CE Primary Academy, Isle Of Grain

Jester

J olly and happy
E xciting and funny
S trong and tall
T all and big
E ntertaining and
R eally funny.

Reggie Trent (6)
St James' CE Primary Academy, Isle Of Grain

In The Sky

I fell through the sky
It was super high.
I landed with a thump
I had an awful bump.
I heard a big shout
When I was out and about.

Blake Lowther (7)
St James' CE Primary Academy, Isle Of Grain

Knight

K eeps enemies out
N ice and strong
I n the castle
G uards
H elmets
T hey ride horses.

Nathan Hill (5)
St James' CE Primary Academy, Isle Of Grain

Knight

K eep enemies out
N ice and strong
I n the castle
G uards
H elmets
T hey ride horses.

Gracie Stewart (5)
St James' CE Primary Academy, Isle Of Grain

King

K ings are bossy and kind
I s the king very powerful?
N ear the kingdom
G reat castle.

Jaiden Reece Cook (6)
St James' CE Primary Academy, Isle Of Grain

King

K eeps people safe
I ncredibly bossy
N ear the castle
G listening crown.

Mitchell Mills (6)
St James' CE Primary Academy, Isle Of Grain

Red, Angry Lolly!

A red, angry lolly was trapped in a cheese ball.
For many years, he shouted for help,
But no one could hear his call.
He could make out in the distance a faraway land,
Could he see a cactus and maybe some sand?
He breathed hot fire to try and set himself free,
With an enormous huff and a puff,
His escape plan was meant to be!
Finally, the red, angry lolly was so happy! Hooray!
But, as the sun shone brightly, he melted away...

Roman Walmsley (8)
St Peter's Catholic Primary School, Sittingbourne

Unicorn Trouble

I was hiring someone to be a unicorn vet.
I said, "Make sure you dry it properly,
They can't fly when they're wet!"
The trainee looked at me with a smile,
But I realised she was in denial.
I said, "Don't be in denial about the unicorn
And don't you forget to polish her horn!"
The trainee polished the horn,
The magic made her shrink,
She realised, if she wanted to be tall,
She'd have to eat something pink!
The trainee summoned a bee
And jumped onto its back, now she could see!
The bee took her to a field and found a pink daisy,
As she picked the petal, she felt a bit lazy.
She got back to the stable and said bye to the bee,
She ate the petal and said, "Oh deary me."
She held her breath and closed her eyes,
As she grew back to her normal size.
She continued polishing the unicorn's horn

And the magic made her shrink.
She said, "Why oh why didn't I think?"

Daisy Kavanagh Williams (7)
St Peter's Catholic Primary School, Sittingbourne

Sleeping On The Moon

It was a dark, stormy night,
I saw nothing but the moon, shining bright.
I wished, one day, I could fly to the moon,
Hopefully, it would happen soon.

"Oh, what is happening now?"
Something was pulling me up, but how?
I had no wings,
Or any other things,
To lift me up into the sky.
I was getting higher and higher,
I was really high.
I saw flowers as blue as the deep ocean,
I saw a lake as pink as a magical potion.
I saw birds with feathers as soft as a cloud,
I heard the squirrels singing very loud.

I heard someone calling my name,
Over and over again,
It was a familiar noise.
Was it my mum's voice?

With a morning sunshine beam,
I realised it was all a dream.
Thank you Moon, my friend,
I hope our friendship will never end.

Emilia Gargula (9)

St Peter's Catholic Primary School, Sittingbourne

Dangerous Dragon!

The bloodthirsty dragon was approaching!
Her feet stomped through the dark cave
As heavy as a mountain!
Her wings opened wide, ready to take off
As fast as a tornado!
She would eat anything in her path!
Her body was scaly and sequined!
She used her brightly patterned body
To reflect at night to see her prey!
Be warned - run and hide away!

Tegan Chapell (8)
St Peter's Catholic Primary School, Sittingbourne

Potions

A potion has bubbles, sometimes smelling so bad,
Most times, they have a good texture,
Sometimes they make you mad.
It never really comes out well
And that can make you sad.
Sometimes, when you mix it,
It goes *pop! Boom! Bang!*
And sometimes, you don't even hear a bell ring.

Chidimma Julia Nwokedi (7)
St Peter's Catholic Primary School, Sittingbourne

Stars

I see a star shining,
It's glittery too.
The world is beautiful,
With stars.
Make a wish with a shooting star,
And it will always come true.
They're golden as well.

Niamh Amalie-Rose Thomason (7)
St Peter's Catholic Primary School, Sittingbourne

Amelia And Her Sweets Living With Her Dragon

Amelia loves sweets, especially her sweet leaf
But she doesn't know what they do to your teeth.

She loves her sweets in her beautiful land
She loves her sweets, so don't touch or she'll hit your hand!

Her pet dragon, with a snort, began to roar
He became tired and he started to snore.

He woke up with his mouth shut,
He tried to stand, but scratched his butt!

All of a sudden, he found a lollipop
But then he started to flop.

She put her hand in his ear and out came a sweet
It was time for him to eat!

Pedetin Hillary Sarah Toyeme (10)
Temple Hill Primary Academy, Dartford

My Friend Is A Bull

My friend is a bull,
He makes us pull,
I heard he dashed so quickly,
He hit Nick,
Nick flew into the sky,
My friend shouted, "Bye-bye!"
When anyone moans,
He groans.

He attacks in a flash,
Going *slash! Slash!*
And if he gives you a smash,
You will have a horrible rash.

My friend is a bull,
Now you know,
He is stronger than metal,
But in the night, he gives a green glow,
He would love a petal,
Some say, "Wow!"
While others say, "Ow!"

Prathyush Policepatil (10)
Temple Hill Primary Academy, Dartford

An Hour Of My Day!

My day starts off with breakfast
And for breakfast, there are toenails
But not just any toenails!
These belong to a donkey!

After that meal, I feel a bit queasy
So I go to poo on a rainbow!
My belly feels free and I feel free
To go and have a dance party!

My party goes well on a cookie
It really helps me release some stress.
I go back home to check the time
It's only been an hour!

Rihanna Usman (9)
Temple Hill Primary Academy, Dartford

Odd One Out

This poem has no point,
But, at the same time, this is unique.
This poem does not rhyme,
This poem took time.
I don't mind.
This is simple,
This is odd,
This is original.
Is it crazy to not have a crazy idea?
Is it not?

Write a haiku,
Write a poem:
Acrostic,
Limerick
Ode,
Villanelle,
Epic,
Distich
Elegy,
Sestina,
Blank verse,

Paradelle,
Qasida,
Rondel,
Sijo,
Which one did I do?

Kristina Lapacka (10)
Temple Hill Primary Academy, Dartford

Nymphadora

I had a cat called Dora
She jumped from sofa to sofa
She ran at the window
And knocked herself out
But got up when I pulled out a banana.

Nymphadora would fight with the dog
She'd nibble on her ear in the night
But when the dog growled
She'd jump in the air and land on my brother's
head.

McKenzie Nicky Allan (9)
Temple Hill Primary Academy, Dartford

Winter Wonderland

Inspired by 'Winter Wonderland' by Joseph T. Renaldi

There are strange and mysterious sounds
When the winter wind blows.
The rustle of the crisp brown leaves
Can be heard through the dark winter mist.
The horses can be heard
Out grazing on the frozen, glistening grass.
People are happy and full of cheer
At this wonderful, magical time of year.

Harvey Rose (9)
Temple Hill Primary Academy, Dartford

YOUNG WRITERS INFORMATION

We hope you have enjoyed reading this book – and that you will continue to in the coming years.

If you're a young writer who enjoys reading and creative writing, or the parent of an enthusiastic poet or story writer, do visit our website **www.youngwriters.co.uk**. Here you will find free competitions, workshops and games, as well as recommended reads, a poetry glossary and our blog. There's lots to keep budding writers motivated to write!

If you would like to order further copies of this book, or any of our other titles, then please give us a call or visit **www.youngwriters.co.uk**.

Young Writers
Remus House
Coltsfoot Drive
Peterborough
PE2 9BF
(01733) 890066
info@youngwriters.co.uk

Join in the conversation!
Tips, news, giveaways and much more!